YOUR KNOWLEDGE HAS VALUE

- We will publish your bachelor's and master's thesis, essays and papers

- Your own eBook and book - sold worldwide in all relevant shops

- Earn money with each sale

Upload your text at www.GRIN.com and publish for free

Bibliographic information published by the German National Library:

The German National Library lists this publication in the National Bibliography; detailed bibliographic data are available on the Internet at http://dnb.dnb.de .

Imprint:

Copyright © 2013 GRIN Verlag, Open Publishing GmbH
Print and binding: Books on Demand GmbH, Norderstedt Germany
ISBN: 978-3-668-10437-2

This book at GRIN:

http://www.grin.com/en/e-book/215695/information-systems-strategy-the-case-of-inked-apparel

Richardson Steve

Information Systems Strategy. The Case of Inked Apparel

GRIN Publishing

GRIN - Your knowledge has value

Since its foundation in 1998, GRIN has specialized in publishing academic texts by students, college teachers and other academics as e-book and printed book. The website www.grin.com is an ideal platform for presenting term papers, final papers, scientific essays, dissertations and specialist books.

Visit us on the internet:

http://www.grin.com/

http://www.facebook.com/grincom

http://www.twitter.com/grin_com

INFORMATION SYSTEM STRATEGY
EBSY601

Inked Apparel

Contents

Organisation

INKEDAPPAREL

[1]

Introduction to organisation

Inked Apparel is a custom clothing manufacturer and retailer; it is primarily situated in two sectors of trading, which is providing a service to its customer by creating a t-shirt of their desire and eventually retailing the produced clothing online as well as at local market stalls.

Inked Apparel is a small business that will create custom T-shirts, Polo's and Hoodies with the choice of customer's preference of images, which can be then created by Ink's design team. These designs can be printed on the back or front as well as both sides of the clothing. Customers request through a form which is available on Ink's website and can be printed in paper form. Once the apparel has been created the company sells it to the customer at an agreed price set beforehand. In addition a market stall is used to help sell generalised merchandise created by the artists for tourists and citizens such as 'I heart London' Shirts; below is an example:

---

[1] Mohammed Arshad 'Inked Apparel' Logo, Designed by Mohammed Date : 1/12/2012

[2] Mohammed Arshad 'Inked Apparel I heart London shirt', Designed by Mohammed Date: 25/11/2012

Business Model Canvas

Key Partners	Key Activities	Value propositions	Customer relationships	Customer Segments
Local market owner allows sales to be taken place at a stall for a fee. **Designers** – creating concepts to be placed into apparel as well as fulfilling customer requests. **Clothing suppliers** – supplies plain t-shirts, hoodies and polo's of our choice	**Customer relationships** – communication skills **Platform and network activity** for interaction.	**Risk reduction** – direct speech to designer for fewer mishaps in design flaw **Usability** – relationship and engaging experience **Design** – varying amount of design choices and designers for needs. **Status** – unique clothing for you to suit your style, and can be limited edition or just for you.	**Co Creation** – specification and design **Automated Services** – website checkout system **Dedicated designer** – custom order fulfilment **Facebook, Twitter, WWW**	**Niche market** – customer unique fashion, own creation **Segmented market** – customer orders and premade apparel. **Important customers**
	Key resources **Intellectual property** – brand, copyright and data. **Hardware and software** - work machines		*Channels* **Facebook, twitter, WWW** **Video call, Phone call.Application form.** **Business flyers.** **Purchase at stalls or internet.** **Delivery via royal mail or secondary delivery service.**	Schools, Universities, Cosplay, Events, Movies

Cost Structure	Revenue streams
Fixed costs- utilities, salary, rent, domain name **Value driven** – focusing on design quality **Cost driven** – low price value proposition	**Dynamic pricing** for custom orders, negotiation. **Fixed Pricing** – list price. **Product sales,** advertising revenue.

Competitors

Inked Apparel has competitors which offer a service of creating t-shirts, they exclusively operate online only, and one of the competitors is branded 'Red Bubble':

Red Bubble http://www.redbubble.com/[3]

Red bubble is a company which allows an artist to upload their designs to sell to customers at a fee much like eBay thus employing an online auction business model. Red bubble provides their customers with an outlet and free advertising. The competition is immense as anyone can upload their designs to sell to their niche – we can use this for ourselves and make an outlet shop on red bubble.

The biggest competitor Inked Apparel faces and one that they inspire to become and more which is:

Street Shirts www.Streetshirts.co.uk[4]

---

[3]Redbubble (2013) *Art Gallery & Community - T-Shirts, Posters, Greeting Cards, Wall Art, Fine Art Prints, Calendars & More | Redbubble*. [online] Available at: http://www.Redbubble.com [Accessed: 2 Apr 2013].

Street Shirts is similar to Inked Apparels business model which is to allow customers to create custom created clothing, however there is a notable difference between the two which is the ability of the customer to request and ask a designer specifically what they desire to be created on their apparel from 'scratch', on street shirts you are able to upload an image and apply it on virtual clothing to give you an idea of what you are purchasing.

Street Shirts specialize in creating their own application software embedded on to their website to make custom apparel to on the user's computer.

Mission Statement

Inked apparel aims to provide a service to take ideas of customers and aim to make them true and existing for them to enjoy. Inked Apparel aims to create designs which will help make clothes more personal for its customers and allow them to express their idea of fashion and their unique style. Inked apparel offers a niche were customers can ask for popular memes or franchise icons to be uniquely drawn for them on the clothing; for example famous quotes such as 'how you doin?' from popular TV shows such as Friends, these unique designs will eventually be available for all customers to purchase with their own imprint.

Goals

- To be an established brand in the UK within 5 years much like what Moonpig did with custom cards.
- Increase clothing ranges from t-shirts, polo's and hoodies.
- To achieve a good cash flow for artist and owner to earn a decent living
- Maintain a solid market share to hold on to and target the right trends and audience
- To create a good network that will allow the expansion of the business
- To establish a work schedule that helps the business operate at optimum
- To build a reputation with quality service and products

Business Strategy

Inked apparel strategy is part of differentiation, cost focus and segmentation.

Differentiation in terms of offering features onto t-shirts and apparel such as logo design onto meeting customer preferences.

Cost is acceptable as it is negotiable as well as producing at lowest possible cost because of the wide accessibility of suppliers for plain shirts.

Segmentation as the clothing is tailored for unique niche market instead of having to serve all customers.

---

[4]Winn, S. (2002) *T-shirt Printing and Custom T-shirts from Streetshirts.* [online] Available at: http://StreetShirts.co.uk [Accessed: 2 Apr 2013].

Task 2

Emerging Technology

Social Messaging Apps & Applications

Social messaging apps developed for iOS and Android phones are quickly becoming a new trend for every user of a mobile phone to effortlessly install applications such as 'Whatsapp' on to their phones for simple and free use. Social messaging apps are building on the success from Blackberry messenger service (bbm) which had great success claiming up to 70 million subscribers according to an article by the guardian[5]. However people and companies have adapted the concept and have made it their own, packing different features as well as being free for the most popular phones on the market such as the IPhone and Samsung Galaxy.

Social messaging apps are a growing trend in technology worldwide as many messaging apps across the world grow rapidly in terms of subscribers. Below is a graph of NHN Line messaging app in Japan which holds 40 million subscribers currently and enjoyed rapid growth.

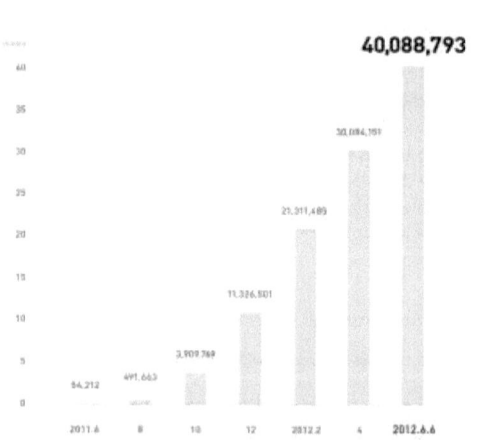

Social messaging applications have heavy implications in terms of the impact it has on mobile operators and competitive social network sites such as Facebook and Twitter. In a recent article by the BBC it is stated that "mobile operators lost $13.9bn"[7] in SMS revenue which implicates a huge market of customers are using social messaging to interact with friends and an income is being saved by millions.

[5] Arthur, C. (2011) *BlackBerry service crash affects BBM messaging for millions.* [online] Available at: http://www.guardian.co.uk/technology/2011/oct/10/blackberry-outage-affects-bbm-services [Accessed: 2 Apr 2013].

[6] Martin, R. (2012) *NHN's Line App Passes 40 Million Users in 1 Year, Looks to Grow as Platform.* [online] Available at: http://www.techinasia.com/line-japan-40-million/ [Accessed: 2 Apr 2013].

[7] BBC News (2012) *Text apps 'lost networks $13.9bn'.* [online] Available at: http://www.bbc.co.uk/news/technology-17111044 [Accessed: 2 Apr 2013].

Social networks such as Facebook have been lacking presence in Asian markets as other social media apps dominate the market as stated in Digital Trends[8]"What's threatening to Facebook is that now with a comfortable foothold in the Asian markets where Facebook lags behind" the article goes on to say that popular applications such as Tango and Line have been dominating the Asian markets and are looking to further their prosperity in the European markets, these companies are looking to expand and creating new offerings to gain a market share.

Inked apparel can use the growth and wealth of applications for mobiles as an advantage to help their position in the market. Social messaging is just an example of the wealth, the communication and exchange of information can help Inked Apparel in terms of the exchange of opinions, videos and pictures as the demographic Inked apparel is very active in this community.

Suitability

Inked apparel can see the growth in applications and especially social media applications as an opportunity to grasp onto as it is evident that there has been substantial growth in this market. In the future if the opportunity may subside as the market becomes saturated, for example WhatsApp has been reaching over 2billion text messages being sent each day, thus receiving the nickname "The SMS killer"[9] connoting to a very active community within the social messaging app market.
If Inked Apparel has not grasped onto the idea of expanding into this area, there is a possibility of it becoming a threat, for example if a competitor created an application or something related to the social market first to meet customer needs, the barriers to entry may increase for Inked Apparel to take advantage of a substantial market.

Social messaging apps allow customers to communicate with one another in groups for free, sending images and videos for example. As a result Inked apparel can take this opportunity of free socialising into their hands by creating a mobile application of their own which will allow customers or potential customers to create their own customers t-shirts. An example of a feature in the application can be taking customer images from their phones or create text that they can create onto the apps apparel maker, eventually uploading it to the apparel website to create; or even better creating a checkout onto the application. This may increase revenue as ideas and images can be shared on the social applications where friends and family can exchange opinions to encourage sales to occur potentially.

Basic applications builders have been created by companies to help firms to create an app for their own brand; a good example of a website which allows businesses or anyone for the matter to create applications is 'AppsBar'[10], tutorials have been created to help users to create applications for mobile phones for consumers to use such as on YouTube[11], these tutorials explain the various amount of features that can be created on your personalised application. A good amount of features such as uploading photos, downloading content, checking out products are a great start for Inked

[8]Bea, F. (2013) *Are messaging apps the biggest threat to Facebook? | Digital Trends.* [online] Available at: http://www.digitaltrends.com/mobile/facebook-has-a-new-lease-on-life/ [Accessed: 2 Apr 2013].

[9]Russell, J. (2012) *WhatsApp founder to operators: We're no SMS-killer, we get people hooked on data.* [online] Available at: http://thenextweb.com/mobile/2012/04/04/whatsapp-founder-to-operators-were-no-sms-killer-we-get-people-hooked-on-data/ [Accessed: 2 Apr 2013].

[10]Appsbar.com (2012) *Rated Best App Maker, The Easiest Way to Create an App - appsbar.* [online] Available at: http://www.appsbar.com/ [Accessed: 2 Apr 2013].

[11]YouTube (n.d.) *appsbar.com - How to Build a Free Android, iPhone, Windows, Blackberry, Facebook and HTML5 App..* [online] Available at: http://www.youtube.com/watch?feature=player_embedded&v=Oatucw4hoO0 [Accessed: 2 Apr 2013].

Apparel to start from. The application creators will allow Inked Apparel to spend on a budget that they can afford as a prominent coder in XML, Java, and HTML will not be needed as much as many of the features can be created for free. Features such as uploading photos for example can be easily implemented into an app Inked Apparel would create to allow users to input images from their phone, checking out products for their own convenience is also always a plus.

Mobile applications allow easier access to customers to access business websites, in recent studies conducted by Compuware "85% per cent of customers prefer apps over mobile websites"[12], mobile applications is a growing trend in technology as its more convenient, faster and easier to navigate.

An example of how successful and ever growing the application market has become is Apples App store for various products it has such as the IPhone and the IPad. Apple's CEO Tim Crook stated the App store has 400 million accounts connected with credit cards and has paid over $5billion dollars in pay checks to its developers of applications, as well as expanding to over 120 countries.[13]

Inked Apparel can create a new strategy which focuses on the objective of taking a slice of the market of applications that are currently on tablet computers and mobiles to increase revenue, brand awareness and marketing.

Cloud Computing

Cloud computing is the use of computer resources such as hardware and software, which will be delivered as a service on a network such as the internet. In terms of a business model, it is usually the case of using software as a service (SaaS); users of the 'cloud' are provided access to the applications software and databases.

Cloud computing changes the structure of a business and changes some costs to from capital expenditure to operating expenditure. Furthermore Cloud computing allows a business to be more agile which is imperative for Inked as customers may want changes in design, cloud computing will help this issue.

Many organisations praise cloud computing as an excellent emerging technology "The impact of Cloud computing on IT outsourcing is no doubt significant, Cloud computing represents a fundamental shift in how organizations pay for and access IT services. It has created new opportunities for IT services providers and the outsourcing vendors will have to modify their strategy to take advantage of this new computing paradigm"[14]

There are many success stories of businesses newly employing cloud computing into their strategy and see a significant difference. A good example of this is MedicAnimal, an online vet supplier which claims to have saved "£10,000 a year"[15] by moving its servers to the cloud. Furthermore they go on

---

[12]Bindi, T. (2012) » *Why more businesses need mobile apps Dynamic Business*. [online] Available at: http://www.dynamicbusiness.com.au/news/why-smbs-need-more-mobile-apps-25032013.html [Accessed: 2 Apr 2013].

[13]Mashable.com (n.d.) Untitled. [online] Available at: http://mashable.com/2012/06/11/wwdc-2012-app-store-stats/ [Accessed: 2 Apr 2013].

[14] SubhankarDhar, (2012) "From outsourcing to Cloud computing: evolution of IT services", Management Research Review, Vol. 35 Iss: 8, pp.664 – 675.

[15] Computerweekly.com (2013) *Top 10 IT strategies for smaller businesses*. [online] Available at: http://www.computerweekly.com/news/1280094155/Top-10-IT-strategies-for-smaller-businesses [Accessed: 2 Apr 2013].

to say purchasing software and hardware outright is a requires significant investment and "it's not an asset worth putting into from a business point of view, as it depreciates so quickly" which does make sense as signing a contract is a cheaper way to allow Inked Apparel receive premium service much earlier in their establishment, rather than waiting for capital.

Suitability

Inked apparel can use cloud computing for the following:

- Reduce overall costs
- Flexibility
- Speed & agility
- Increase global reach

Reduce overall costs: Inked apparel overall costs will reduce as the efficiency of designs and creating clothing will increase which will help lower costs. Cloud computing allows you to use full featured, highly distributed platforms and software's to use, which can give Inked access to greater products to help in creating better quality goods.

Flexibility: Flexibility will increase in Inked in terms of operation as currently having idle resources is not efficient such as in a time of lower sales, however in cloud computing dealing with limited capacity or running out of capacity and eventually giving customer a poor experience is made smaller risk, because cloud computing you are allowed easily receive more capacity if you require it by using the provision system.

Speed and agility: The cloud computing environment changes how you are able to develop and deploy your creation and allow your team to experiment more often.

Increase global reach: Inked apparel may have potential around the world; there is no way of knowing where demand is needed across the globe unless you try. It is difficult to distribute your reach globally as most start-up businesses or smaller firms focus on the local geographic regions. However cloud computing will allow Inked to have the potential to employ designers worldwide which can then access their 'world' and help communication between the two

Task 3

There are many different tools for strategic analysis of a business, I will choose Critical Success Factor and Porters five forces analysis as they provide a clear concise overview of what needs to be done and how it can be achieved.

Porters five forces (Appendix 1)

Porters five forces was developed by Michael Porter and allows us "to assess the possible impact of IS on the competitive position of the firm"[16], porters five forces framework also allows "IS represent a opportunity to secure a strategic advantage by using to strengthen one of more of these forces"[17], thus allowing Inked Apparel to know which one of these forces will need to be strengthened.

Check Appendix 1

Critical Success Factor (Appendix 2)

Critical success factor will allow inked apparel "gain commitment to contribute achievement in critical area" - Ward, J and Peppard J. (2002)[18].

Critical success factor allows us to understand the key factors needed for inked apparel which is in the clothing industry is to meet customer desires which can derive from trends media have set to become popular. In addition having to establish a efficient work schedule which will eventually increase customer satisfaction of service. Last innovation will need to take place to take advantage of merging technologies such as applications to increase brand awareness and market share.

The critical success factor is located in the Appendix.

Business Process of Inked Apparel

A business process is defined as a chronological order of activities that will turn inputs into outputs; they usually consist of the following:

- A starting and ending point
- Inputs and outputs
- Activities that transform the inputs into an output
- A metric for measuring effectiveness.[19]

Examples of a metric that will help measure effectiveness are customer satisfaction, quality of products produced and profit per output.

---

[16] Boddy, D., &Boonstra, A. (2009).*Managing information systems: strategy and organisation*. Harlow, FT Prentice Hall. Page 71

[17] Boddy, D., &Boonstra, A. (2009).*Managing information systems: strategy and organisation*. Harlow, FT Prentice Hall. Page 71

[18] Ward, J., &Peppard, J. (2002).*Strategic planning for information systems*.Chichester, West Sussex, England, J. Wiley. http://search.ebscohost.com/login.aspx?direct=true&scope=site&db=nlebk&db=nlabk&AN=81181, 3rd Edition, Page 126

[19] University of Westminster Information Technology Strategy Lecture 4 Page 3

An example of a business process:

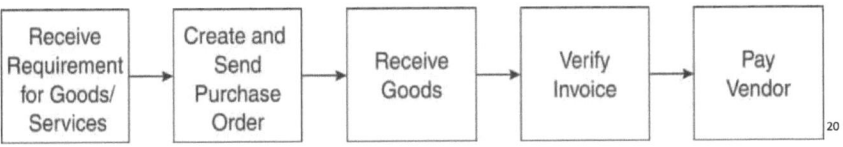

Examples of Business processes for Inked Apparel include fulfilling customer orders, manufacturing the t-shirts, planning and design.

Inked Apparel Processes for customer orders:

1)

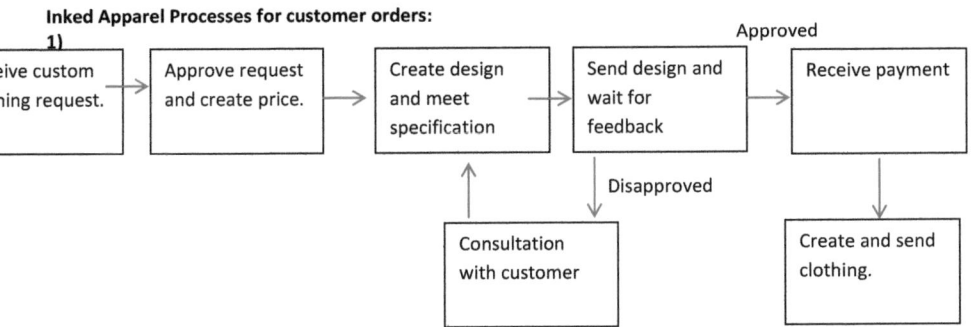

Inked Apparel process for manufacturing

2)

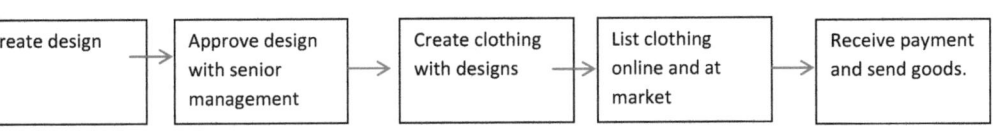

Delegation of work

3)

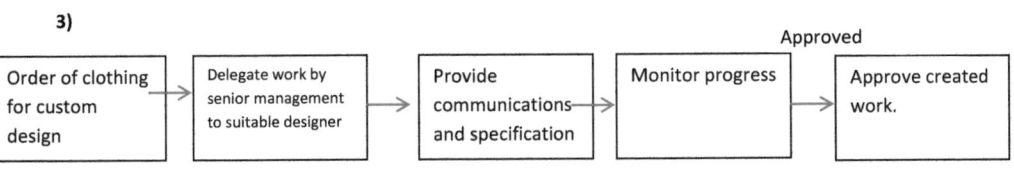

These are key examples of processes currently at Inked apparel that can addressed in multiple ways to improve, for example doing a systematic redesign or starting with a clean sheet.

---

[20] Pearlson, K. and Saunders, C. (2012) Strategic Management of Information Systems, 5/e, Wiley

A systematic redesign asks the following questions:

"Is it possible to eliminate process steps?
Many processes contain unnecessary steps and cause unnecessary waiting times
•Is it possible to simplify process steps?
E.g. unnecessary forms/procedures. Use of internet?
•Is it possible to integrate process steps?
E.g. can you reduce the number of people or departments involved?
•Is it possible to automate process steps?
E.g. Can duplication of data capture or transfer be eliminated?"[21]

Inked Apparel does show problem of flow with certain processes such as delegation of work as well as the requirement of consulting the customer for redesigning, this can become time consuming and not cost effective for the business as it is not efficient.

A few things Inked Apparel can consider are enterprise systems which will allow information to flow between the processes such as delegating work to a suitable designer.

Customer relationship management systems

A customer relationship management system is strongly suggested to Inked Apparel as it seems to be a very social company and a lot of interaction is needed between the customer and business.

Many customer relationship management systems are subscription based such as Cloud Computing which I strongly suggested earlier something Inked Apparel should take up on.

CRM will help lead to better customer service, better communication, more simplified sales and can possible increase revenue.

The era of the "social customer"[22] is increase with the use of social apps, twitter, Facebook and LinkedIn. The CRM based strategy incorporates these networks and communities into their model.

The benefits of incorporating Enterprise system to Inked Apparel:

- Elimination of redundant processes
- Elimination of redundant data
- Elimination of redundant design creations
- Elimination of delegation of work, increase efficiency
- New standards of procedure can be created which allow easier communication between parties and efficiently.
- Standard interface which is familiar.

The Disadvantage of incorporating CRM:

- Change in organisation structure, can trouble employees.
- Subscription, more operational costs
- Staff may need training to use the system
- First few weeks of integration will be risky

---

[21] Boddy, D., Boonstra, A., & Kennedy, G. (2009), Managing Information Systems: Strategy and Organisation, 3rd Edition, Prentice Hall

[22] Greenberg, Paul (2009). *CRM at the Speed of Light* (4th ed.). McGraw Hill.p. 7.

Inked apparel may also face challenges for integrating a CRM system into their businesses such as the security and legal issues with sharing, protection and integrity of the data provided by customers. Standards set by the company will have to be created or industry standards and guidelines must be abided to.

Organisation structure

Inked Apparel operates in a decentralized architecture environment. This involves arranging hardware, software, networking and data on multiple computers and devices, which in Inked situation is every designer's computer and workstations operated by admins. A decentralised architecture allows Inked to have greater flexibility and technology installed on personal computers can be customized which is ideal for designers to suit their environment.

However this can create some problems such as delegation, tracking and organisation of work across the business. Therefore a new infrastructure for the business which can be employed is virtual cloud computing or SaaS services.

Benefits of virtualization and cloud computing:

•Consolidated physical servers.
•Reduced physical costs of the data centre.
•No upgrading
•No maintenance, power, or electricity costs.
•No need for physical space or storage servers.
•*Increased speed of attaining additional capacity (provisioning).*

Cloud computing provides the option of private clouds which allows data to be managed by the company and remains within the company, which can help with privacy and security issues that inked may face such as revealing company information such as Skype id's which can then be DoS'd by someone.

A primary benefit of incorporating cloud services is agility as it "enables to better predict and respond to market changes and environmental pressure rapidly and with optimal effectiveness"[23] which is relevant to the clothing industry as trends change often.

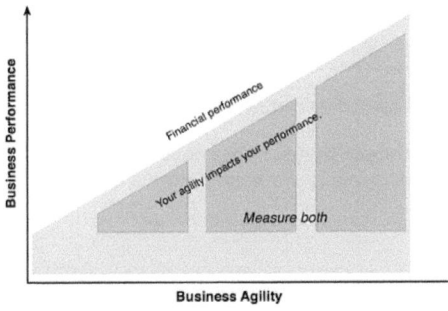

[24]

There is also the question of insourcing or outsourcing.

---

[23] Is Your Company Ready for Cloud?: Choosing the Best Cloud Adoption Strategy ... By Pamela K. Isom, Kerrie Holle
[24] Is Your Company Ready for Cloud?: Choosing the Best Cloud Adoption Strategy ... By Pamela K. Isom, Kerrie Holle

Following the framework in Pearlson and Saunders (2012) books in strategic management:

"Make" or "Buy"	Suggests Insourcing	Suggests Outsourcing	Examples of Associated Risk in Worse Case Scenarios
Questions			
Does it involve a core competency?	Yes	No	*If outsourced:* Loss of control over strategic initiatives; loss of strategic focus
Does it involve confidential or sensitive IS services or software development?	Yes	No	*If outsourced:* Competitive secrets may be leaked
Is there enough time available to complete software development projects in-house?	Yes	No	*If insourced:* Project not completed on time
Do the in-house IS professionals have adequate training, experience, or skills to provide the service or develop the software?	Yes	No	*If outsourced:* Technological innovations limited to what provider offers; overreliance on provider's skills
Are there reliable outsourcing providers who are likely to stay in business for the duration of the contract?	No	Yes	*If outsourced:* Project not completed, or, if completed, project is over budget and late when another provider takes it over

25

Is there an outsourcing provider that has a culture and practices that are compatible with the client?	No	Yes	*If outsourced:* Conflict between client and provider personnel
Are there economies of scale that make it cheaper to provide the service or develop the software in-house?	Most Likely No	Most Likely Yes	*If outsourced:* Costs of project or operations becomes excessive because of the way the contract is written
Does it offer a better ability to handle peaks?	Most Likely No	Most Likely Yes	*If insourced:* Loss of business
Does it involve consolidating data centers?	Most Likely No	Most Likely Yes	*If insourced:* Inefficient operations

Applying the framework to Inked Apparel, it is suggested that insourcing should be taken upon.

However Inked apparel is using selective outsourcing or 'strategic outsourcing' where an organisation chooses which IT capabilities to retain in-house and which to outsource.

---

[25] Pearlson, K. and Saunders, C. (2012) Strategic Management of Information Systems, 4/e, Wiley, Chapter 7, 8 **Make or buy? Questions and risks (pp 265)**

Resources[26]

This table illustrates the resources Inked Apparel will require to implement the new strategy being proposed and what changes may be needed.

Component	What		Who		Where	
	Infrastructure	**Architecture**	**Infrastructure**	**Architecture**	**Infrastructure**	**Architecture**
Hardware	1TB Hard drives recommended(500GB Minimum)	Windows Operated systems Dell Alien wares or IOS Macs (employee preference).	Owner of the business will provide hardware to all partners.	The IT support for their hardware will be the responsibility of the partners.	N/A	Distributed Servers
Software	ERP, CRM. Modules for: communication, design, sales, accounting.	CRM software	Employees may need training with new system	Designers will be most affected by the changes	SaaS services.	N/A
Network	Provide employees with ISP contracts if needed.	Unlimited bandwidth ISP with no fair usage policy will be ideal, may need leased lines at times of high sales.	Current ISP is BT; deal must be created to follow provision of staff.	All employees employed by inked apparel will need a connection.	Cable modem to ISP, Routers, Firewalls and repeaters.	Cable modem to ISP, Routers, Firewalls and repeaters.
Data	Customer information address and requirements.	Database: MySQL, access or saas systems. Databases for Sales and accounting.	Password protection, only authorised users can access the system.	Designers will only have access to their custom design tasks, admins will have access to everything.	Data will be on the cloud and backed up into mySql also.	Backups will be done online.

Evaluation of Proposals

There are two main proposals for Inked Apparel to create a new strategy which are to indulge in two new emerging technologies which have substantial growth with healthy market and revenue streams.

Inked Apparel can either create a new application for mobile operating systems to help them market to a wider audience and potentially increase revenue as the mobile market soars to billions of dollars as predictions are set for the market to hit "46$billion by 2016"[27], however it is stated the vast majority of revenue is being made by "highly committed mobile gamers" as they purchase most frequently. Therefore the characteristics of Inked business may not exactly meet the requirements, however with application builders being out there, it is always a possibility as a prominent coder will

---

[26] Pearlson, K. and Saunders, C. (2012) Strategic Management of Information Systems, 5/e (or 4/e) Wiley Page 179

[27] CNET (2012) Mobile app revenue set to soar to $46 billion in 2016. [online] Available at: http://news.cnet.com/8301-13506_3-57379364-17/mobile-app-revenue-set-to-soar-to-$46-billion-in-2016/ [Accessed: 2 Apr 2013].

not be needed to create one; however it will be lacking as it will be generic to many other apps that have been created with application builders, as a result not gain much attention.

The second proposal is for Inked Apparel to use cloud computing, which is another emerging technology which has many great successes to businesses such as Google, Amazon and Dropbox. An example of success with the use of cloud computing can also be seen through Haven power[28] which has employed amazon cloud services in which they had problems in disc space and servers, however with the new strategy of cloud computing Haven as said "we now have the capability of inhousing" as well as having no problems with the new system.

Inked apparel already employs a decentralised structure in their business model, this may help in the adaptation into employing a virtual cloud sourcing architecture they have familiar characteristics, however being more organised and professional for example relying on a network to be connected to each other, the environment in which the staff will work in will seem familiar.

Providers of cloud computing include Salesforce, Concor and Transversal. Within a cloud model there are risks that small to medium sides businesses may face. A major concern is making the functions within the cloud model to increase the business in flexibility. The aim of employing cloud computing is to "provide the business components that can be brought together as required in what are called "composite applications" and this requires a deep understanding how different functions need to interopete"[29] it is recommended therefore that cloud providers themselves such as Salesforce provide a platform to make things more easier and reasonable.

However the benefits do outweigh the disadvantages of using cloud computing as it will provide Inked with numerous benefits such as reducing costs and allowing a better relationship to be developed between employees and managerial positions as work will have a greater flow. Therefore this strategy is a clear winner to be as an opportunity to the company.

---

[28]Computerweekly.com (2013) *Case study: Energy firm scales IT through Amazon Web Services cloud*. [online] Available at: http://www.computerweekly.com/news/2240106560/Case-study-Energy-firm-scales-IT-through-Amazon-Web-Services-cloud [Accessed: 2 Apr 2013].

[29]Computerweekly.com (2013) *What are the outsourcing options for the SME?*. [online] Available at: http://www.computerweekly.com/feature/What-are-the-options-for-an-SMB-when-it-comes-to-outsourcing [Accessed: 2 Apr 2013].

Appendix

SWOT

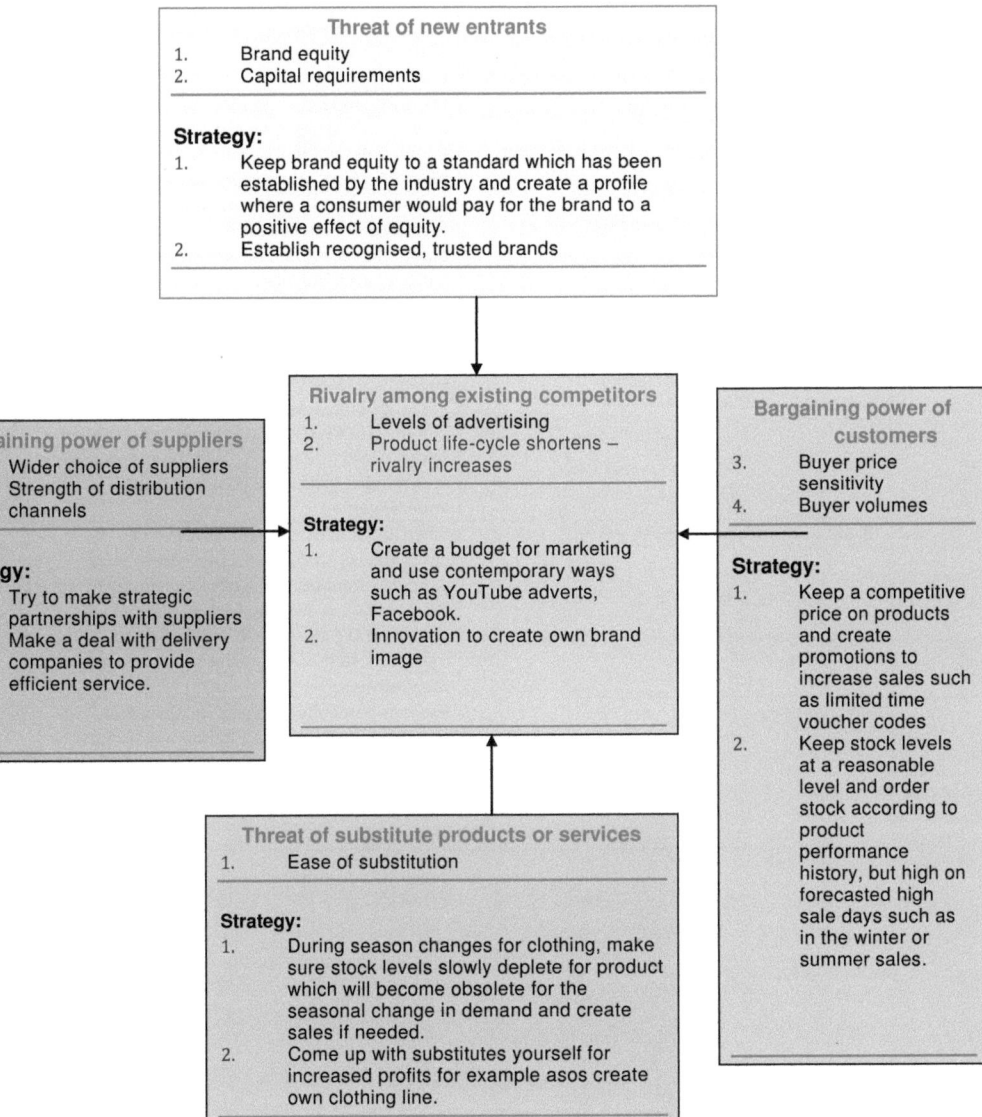

Threat of new entrants
1. Brand equity
2. Capital requirements

Strategy:
1. Keep brand equity to a standard which has been established by the industry and create a profile where a consumer would pay for the brand to a positive effect of equity.
2. Establish recognised, trusted brands

Rivalry among existing competitors
1. Levels of advertising
2. Product life-cycle shortens – rivalry increases

Strategy:
1. Create a budget for marketing and use contemporary ways such as YouTube adverts, Facebook.
2. Innovation to create own brand image

rgaining power of suppliers
Wider choice of suppliers
Strength of distribution channels

tegy:
Try to make strategic partnerships with suppliers
Make a deal with delivery companies to provide efficient service.

Bargaining power of customers
3. Buyer price sensitivity
4. Buyer volumes

Strategy:
1. Keep a competitive price on products and create promotions to increase sales such as limited time voucher codes
2. Keep stock levels at a reasonable level and order stock according to product performance history, but high on forecasted high sale days such as in the winter or summer sales.

Threat of substitute products or services
1. Ease of substitution

Strategy:
1. During season changes for clothing, make sure stock levels slowly deplete for product which will become obsolete for the seasonal change in demand and create sales if needed.
2. Come up with substitutes yourself for increased profits for example asos create own clothing line.

Competitive force	Application of force to Inked Apparel
Threats of New entrants	Inked Apparel offers a group of designers to customers to meet styles, fashion, and vision. New entrants are unlikely to provide a supportive relationship between customer and business, as inked apparel makes the design of clothes more personal.
Bargaining Power of Customers	Inked Apparel has a monthly cycle of creating new product designs for customers to purchase. Previous designs will be on sale as well which will boast a wide product range. Some clothing may be limited edition and stock may be low therefore will entice customers to purchase before they are gone. Recently Inked Apparel is looking into more inked transfer method for higher quality products.
Bargaining Power of Suppliers	Many suppliers work is relatively easy for the requirements inked apparel needs. This pool of suppliers is large thus the supplier should have a great flexibility towards Inked Apparel to keep a healthy relationship. Season changes and color schemes will be dependent on the supplier being able to fulfill the needs, thus a strong is imperative.
Threat of substitute products	Inked apparel forces the imperative of concentering on customer preferences and desires. Competitors will offer similar quality as the method used for applying the designs to clothing is the same, thus in this industry it is mostly about quality, satisfaction and loyalty of the customer.
Competitors	Inked Apparel offers competitive prices for customers to think about it. However off course some services such as a complete overhaul and custom design of apparel will cost more. Inked apparel hopes the artistic vision of designs will help sales.

CSF

1.

Vision - Mission
Mission: To be an established brand
Vision: Within 5 years be a major contender with street shirts
Strategic Goal
What do we have to do: Understand customer demographic more, investment in growth markets, Strong brand awareness
Strategic Goal: Increase brand awareness and exposure.
Critical Success Factor
How will we get there: Creation of application or software for website or mobile device.
Sustain a healthy customer satisfaction rate

2.

Mission:

Increase clothing ranges from t-shirts, polo's and hoodies.

Critical Success Factors:

- Create healthy relationships with suppliers
- Secure financing for expansion of products

Goals:

- Understand customer desire
- Expand product range to attract more sales and customers
- Expand stock room for storage space

3

Mission:
Maintain a
solid
market
share

Critical Success Factors:

- Keeping up with trends and flavours of the months
- Discounts and sales for promotional seasons
- Innovation and design style to go 'viral'

Goals:

- Gain a market share locally of 20%
- Being a strong competitor

4

Mission: Work
schedule that
helps the
business operate
at optimum

Critical Success Factors:

- Using motivating techniques to help staff
- Analysis of work rate
- Bonuses for staff

Goals:
- Gain a solid work schedule that is optimum for all staff
- Having a good work turnover and less absenteeism

Bibliography

[1] Mohammed Arshad 'Inked Apparel' Logo, Designed by Mohammed Date : 1/12/2012

[1] Mohammed Arshad 'Inked Apparel I heart London shirt', Designed by Mohammed Date: 25/11/2012

Boddy, D., &Boonstra, A. (2009).*Managing information systems: strategy and organisation*. Harlow, FT Prentice Hall.

Greenberg, P. (2009). *CRM at the speed of light: CRM 2.0 strategies, tools and techniques for engaging your customers*. Emeryville, Calif, McGraw-Hill/Osborne.

Ward, J., &Peppard, J. (2002).*Strategic planning for information systems*.Chichester, West Sussex, England, J. Wiley. http://search.ebscohost.com/login.aspx?direct=true&scope=site&db=nlebk&db=nlabk&AN=81 181.

Is Your Company Ready for Cloud?: Choosing the Best Cloud Adoption Strategy ... By Pamela K. Isom, Kerrie Holle

University of Westminster Information Technology Strategy Lecture 4 Page 3

Appsbar.com (2012) *Rated Best App Maker, The Easiest Way to Create an App - appsbar*. [online] Available at: http://www.appsbar.com/ [Accessed: 2 Apr 2013].

Arthur, C. (2011) *BlackBerry service crash affects BBM messaging for millions*. [online] Available at: http://www.guardian.co.uk/technology/2011/oct/10/blackberry-outage-affects-bbm-services [Accessed: 2 Apr 2013].

BBC News (2012) *Text apps 'lost networks $13.9bn'*. [online] Available at: http://www.bbc.co.uk/news/technology-17111044 [Accessed: 2 Apr 2013].

Bea, F. (2013) *Are messaging apps the biggest threat to Facebook? | Digital Trends*. [online] Available at: http://www.digitaltrends.com/mobile/facebook-has-a-new-lease-on-life/ [Accessed: 2 Apr 2013].

Bindi, T. (2012) *» Why more businesses need mobile apps Dynamic Business*. [online] Available at: http://www.dynamicbusiness.com.au/news/why-smbs-need-more-mobile-apps-25032013.html [Accessed: 2 Apr 2013].

CNET (2012) *Mobile app revenue set to soar to $46 billion in 2016*. [online] Available at: http://news.cnet.com/8301-13506_3-57379364-17/mobile-app-revenue-set-to-soar-to-$46-billion-in-2016/ [Accessed: 2 Apr 2013].

Computerweekly.com (2013) *Top 10 IT strategies for smaller businesses*. [online] Available at: http://www.computerweekly.com/news/1280094155/Top-10-IT-strategies-for-smaller-businesses [Accessed: 2 Apr 2013].

Computerweekly.com (2013) *Case study: Energy firm scales IT through Amazon Web Services cloud*. [online] Available at: http://www.computerweekly.com/news/2240106560/Case-study-Energy-firm-scales-IT-through-Amazon-Web-Services-cloud [Accessed: 2 Apr 2013].

Computerweekly.com (2013) *What are the outsourcing options for the SME?*. [online] Available at: http://www.computerweekly.com/feature/What-are-the-options-for-an-SMB-when-it-comes-to-outsourcing [Accessed: 2 Apr 2013].

Martin, R. (2012) *NHN's Line App Passes 40 Million Users in 1 Year, Looks to Grow as Platform*. [online] Available at: http://www.techinasia.com/line-japan-40-million/ [Accessed: 2 Apr 2013].

Mashable.com (n.d.) *Untitled*. [online] Available at: http://mashable.com/2012/06/11/wwdc-2012-app-store-stats/ [Accessed: 2 Apr 2013].

Redbubble (2013) *Art Gallery & Community - T-Shirts, Posters, Greeting Cards, Wall Art, Fine Art Prints, Calendars & More | Redbubble*. [online] Available at: http://www.Redbubble.com [Accessed: 2 Apr 2013].

Russell, J. (2012) *WhatsApp founder to operators: We're no SMS-killer, we get people hooked on data*. [online] Available at: http://thenextweb.com/mobile/2012/04/04/whatsapp-founder-to-operators-were-no-sms-killer-we-get-people-hooked-on-data/ [Accessed: 2 Apr 2013].

Winn, S. (2002) *T-shirt Printing and Custom T-shirts from Streetshirts*. [online] Available at: http://StreetShirts.co.uk [Accessed: 2 Apr 2013].

YouTube (n.d.) *appsbar.com - How to Build a Free Android, iPhone, Windows, Blackberry, Facebook and HTML5 App.*. [online] Available at: http://www.youtube.com/watch?feature=player_embedded&v=Oatucw4hoO0 [Accessed: 2 Apr 2013].

---

i